What were stocks? Was witchcraft a crime? What were gangsters? What is the scene of the crime? These are just some of the questions answered in this fascinating book.

Find out how crimes and punishments have changed. Read about the extraordinary ways in which people were punished in Greek and Roman times and the methods used today. Discover how courts work and what the judge and jury do.

Packed with facts and colourful illustrations, this book will answer all your questions about crime and punishment through the ages.

4

The earliest known legal text was written in Mesopotamia in about 2100 BC. It was carved on to a tablet of clay.

In Tibet, criminals were sometimes thrown into dungeons to be eaten alive by scorpions.

From ancient times, criminals have been punished for their crimes. Over the years, however, people's ideas of crime and punishment have changed a great deal. Some of the punishments handed out long ago seem very cruel to us today, and some of the crimes very odd indeed.

Q Why were people banished?

A In early times, people lived in groups, called tribes or clans. All the members of a tribe looked after each other and helped each other to find food. The worst form of punishment was to be banished from your tribe. This might happen if you stole from or killed another member of the tribe.

Q What happened to thieves in Ancient Tibet?

A Thieves in Ancient Tibet had to repay the goods they stole, with interest! If they stole from the king, they had to repay the theft 100 times; from a monk, 80 times; and from an ordinary person, nine times.

Q How were Chinese criminals punished?

A During the 3rd century BC, tens of thousands of criminals in Ancient China were put to work building the Great Wall. This huge wall ran for over 9,000 km across the north of China, to keep invaders out of the country.

The Great Wall of China

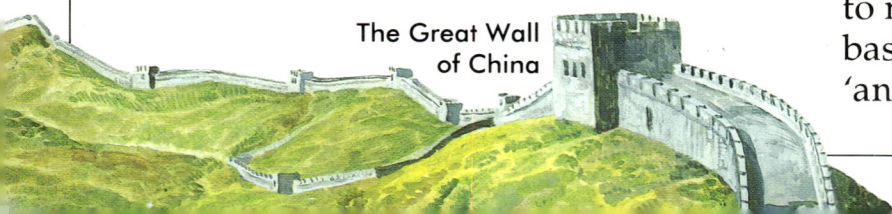

Q What was Hammurabi's code?

A Hammurabi's code was a system of laws set up by King Hammurabi of Babylon in 1758 BC. It was carved on a stone pillar in the temple for all to read. The code was based on the principle of 'an eye for an eye'.

100 QUESTIONS AND ANSWERS

CRIME
AND
PUNISHMENT

Written by
Anita Ganeri

Designed by
Juan Hayward

PUFFIN BOOKS

Consultants:
Richard Tames is a freelance writer,
specialising in history. He has written many
books for children as well as contributions
to encyclopedias.
Simon Heathcote is a police constable with
the West Yorkshire police force.

PUFFIN BOOKS

Published by the Penguin Group
Penguin Books Ltd, 27 Wrights Lane, London W8 5TZ, England
Penguin Books USA Inc., 375 Hudson Street, New York, New York 10014, USA
Penguin Books Australia Ltd, Ringwood, Victoria, Australia
Penguin Books Canada Ltd, 10 Alcorn Avenue, Toronto, Ontario, Canada M4V 3B2
Penguin Books (NZ) Ltd, 182-190 Wairau Road, Auckland 10, New Zealand

Penguin Books Ltd, Registered Offices: Harmondsworth, Middlesex, England

First published 1994
10 9 8 7 6 5 4 3 2 1

Produced for Puffin Books by Zigzag Publishing Ltd,
The Barn, Randolph's Farm, Brighton Road,
Hurstpierpoint, West Sussex BN6 9EL, England

Senior Editor: Philippa Moyle
Managing Editor: Nicola Wright
Production: Zoë Fawcett
Series Concept: Tony Potter
Illustrated by Hemesh Alles, Peter Bull, Peter Dennis,
Philip Hood and Ed Org
Additional illustration: Mainline Design
Cover illustration: David Farren

Colour separations: RCS Graphics, Leeds and Sussex Repro, Brighton, England
Printed by Proost, Belgium

Contents

Ma'at was the Ancient Egyptian goddess of truth and justice. The pharaoh (king) was in charge of law and order on Earth.

The Maya lived in Mexico from the 3rd century BC to the 15th century AD.

Q What was the worst crime in Egypt?

A One of the worst crimes in Ancient Egypt was killing a cat, for which the punishment was instant death. The Ancient Egyptians believed that cats were sacred animals and should be treated with great respect.

Q What happened to bad losers in Mayan times?

A In Mayan times, being bad at sport was a criminal offence. The Maya played their own, very painful, form of basketball. Players could not touch the hard rubber ball with their hands, only with their elbows and hips. The losing team was put to death after a game and their heads displayed on spikes.

Q What was wergeld?

A If a Viking was murdered, the murderer had to pay the victim's family a sum of money representing what the victim was worth. This was called wergeld. It was based on the victim's rank in society.

Q How did the Vikings settle their differences?

A The Vikings had no legal system or police force to keep law and order. Some quarrels were settled by duels which were often fought to the death. The winner was awarded his opponent's property and possessions.

Burglaries were commonplace in Ancient Rome. Wealthy people had fierce guard dogs to protect their homes.

The Ancient Greeks lived about 3,000 years ago. Roman civilisation began about 2,000 years ago. Both had advanced systems of law and order, although some of their punishments seem cruel or unfair to us today. Many modern legal systems are based on Roman law and it is still studied as part of many university law degrees.

Q Which criminals took poison as punishment?

A The Greeks allowed people accused of treason to end their own lives by taking poison. This is what happened to the philosopher, Socrates, in 399 BC. His only crime was speaking out against the government of Athens.

Poisonous hemlock

Q What was 'ostracism'?

A Ostracism was a punishment for Greek politicians who had become unpopular or troublesome. They were banished for 10 years. Once a year, people could vote on who to ostracise. They cast their votes by writing the person's name on a piece of broken pottery (below). At least 6,000 votes were needed to banish a person.

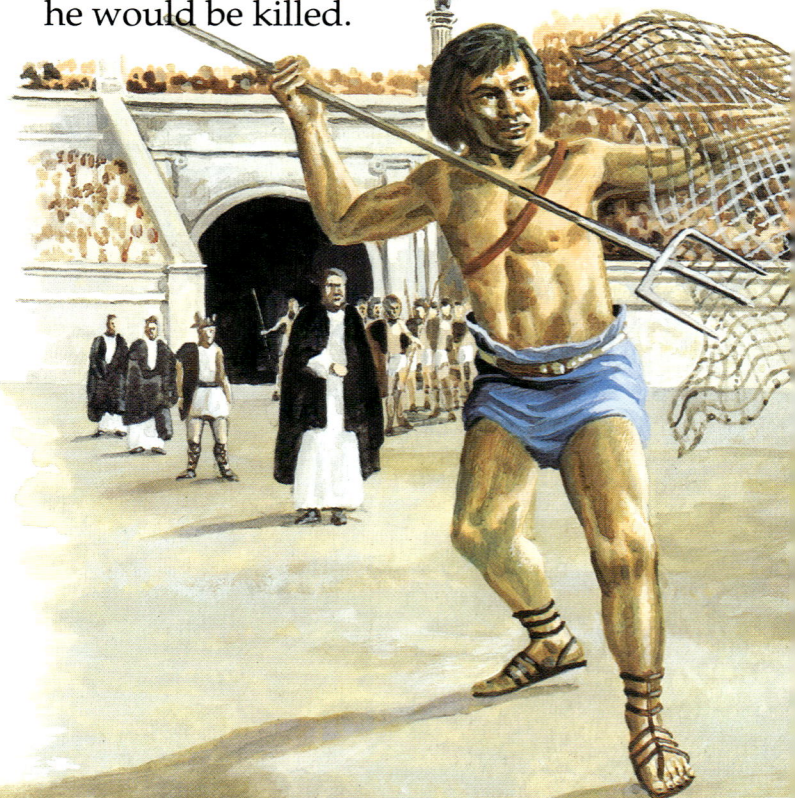

Q Why wouldn't you want to be a Roman gladiator?

A Gladiators were picked from condemned criminals, prisoners of war and slaves. They trained in special gladiator schools. Gladiator fights were hugely popular spectator sports in Ancient Rome. They were usually fought to the death but a wounded gladiator could appeal to the crowd for mercy. 'Thumbs up' meant he would be spared; 'thumbs down' meant he would be killed.

Many Roman criminals were sentenced to be oarsmen on warships. Their lives were made very hard indeed.

Q What was the penalty for killing a father?

A In Roman times, a person found guilty of killing his or her father was put in a sack with a live cock, viper and dog, and drowned in a river.

Q How were crimes punished in the Roman army?

A Very harshly indeed! If a unit of soldiers deserted in battle, the punishment was death by 'decimation'. This meant that one in every 10 of the guilty soldiers was picked out at random and put to death. The remaining soldiers were in disgrace.

Q Who did the Romans crucify?

A Slaves and religious or political trouble-makers were crucified (nailed to a cross and left to die). In AD 30, Jesus Christ was crucified in Jerusalem on the orders of the Roman governor, Pontius Pilate. St Peter was crucified in AD 64 by the Roman emperor, Nero. He asked to be crucified upside-down because he was not worthy to die in the same way as Jesus.

Q What was a Roman court like?

A In Rome, the basilica (a large public building) acted as the law court. Anyone who claimed that a crime had been committed had to summon the suspect to appear at court, even if it took force to get them there. The suspect could pay a lawyer to speak for them. The case was heard before a judge and a jury. The jury decided if the suspect was innocent or guilty. Then the judge passed sentence.

The thumbscrew (far right) was one of the most common instruments of torture in the Middle Ages.

What happened in the Middle Ages?

The Middle Ages is the name given to the period of history in Europe between the 12th and 15th centuries. During this time, the Catholic church became very powerful. Many crimes were considered to be sins and were punished very severely indeed.

Q Why were people tortured?

A People were tortured in order to make them confess to a crime and to name anyone who had helped them. Many extremely cruel forms of torture were used in the Middle Ages. They included the use of thumbscrews, being stretched on a rack and roasting the victim's feet in a fire.

Q What did the Inquisition do?

A The Inquisition was set up by the Pope in the 13th century to search out and punish heretics (people who did not agree with the Church's teachings). People even vaguely suspected of heresy were brought before monks who acted as judges. They were cross-questioned and often tortured. If they were found guilty but repented, they could be sentenced to life imprisonment. If they would not repent, they were burnt at the stake.

Q How could peas prove a person's guilt?

A One of the oddest ways of deciding whether thieves were innocent or guilty was to place a handful of peas on a table under an upturned bowl. Suspects were led to the table, one by one. When the guilty person went to the table, the peas were supposed to bounce up and down!

Q What were stocks?

A A set of stocks was made of two boards, one on top of the other, with two small holes in between. A person sat with his or her ankles through the holes, while bystanders jeered or threw rotten fruit and vegetables. Sitting in the stocks was a common sentence in the Middle Ages.

Q What was coin-clipping and how was it punished?

A To make a bit of extra money, people clipped the edges off real coins and melted them together to make new ones. If they got caught, coin-clippers had their right hands cut off.

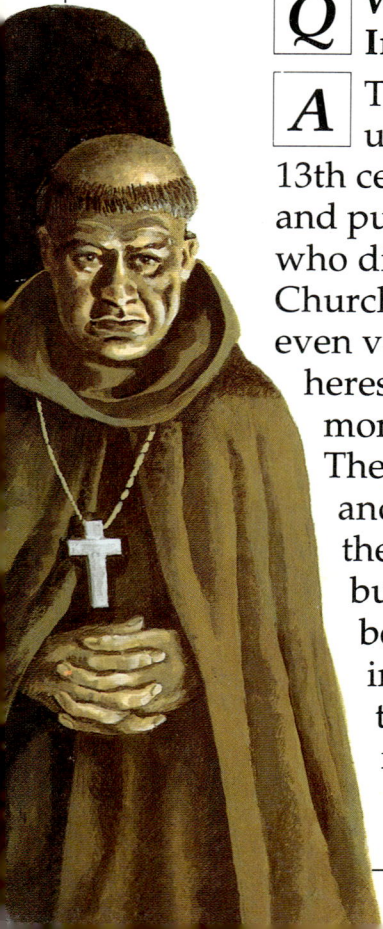

If a fishmonger sold bad fish, he was paraded around town wearing a necklace of smelly, rotten fish!

Guilty men

Q How were criminals judged in the Middle Ages?

A Often by rumour and hearsay! Twelve men were picked from the neighbourhood where the crime was committed. They had to decide, in court, if the suspect was guilty. They did not decide on the basis of any hard evidence but on what they themselves knew of events or on what local people thought had happened.

Q What happened in trial by ordeal?

A Trial by ordeal was a method of trying suspects in the Middle Ages. It took several forms. In trial by cold water, accused people were thrown into a pond or river. If they floated, they were guilty. If they sank, they were judged to be innocent (even though they had probably drowned by this time!).

Q What was trial by boiling water?

A In trial by boiling water, the accused had to plunge his or her arm into boiling water. If he or she didn't get burnt, the verdict was innocent. Not many people were that lucky.

Nagging women wore a 'scold's bridle' (right) — a metal helmet with a piece of iron which pressed the tongue down.

When were criminals executed?

In the 16th and 17th centuries, some crimes, such as witchcraft or high treason (disloyalty to king or country), continued to be punished by death. Lesser punishments included floggings and duckings. Punishments were often carried out in public, as a warning to people to obey the law. Even minor crimes were punished harshly.

Q Why were people flogged?

A People were flogged, or whipped, for a wide range of crimes, including stealing, gambling, being drunk and fighting. As a warning to others, they were whipped in public, through the streets or at a special 'whipping post' in the market place.

Q Which criminals were beheaded?

A People of high rank, such as knights and nobles, and traitors were beheaded for their crimes. Their heads were cut off with an axe or a sword and stuck on spikes to warn others. King Henry VIII of England had two of his six wives, Anne Boleyn and Catherine Howard, beheaded.

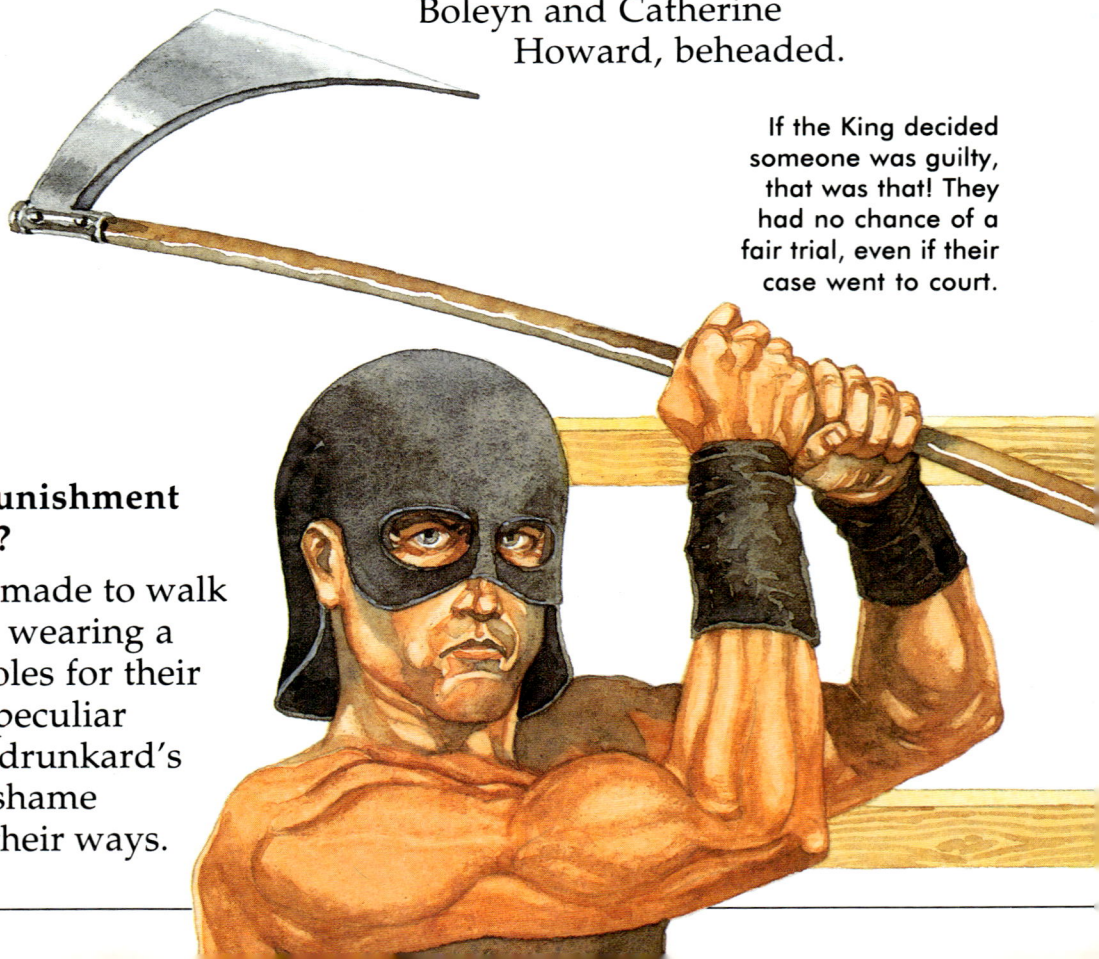

If the King decided someone was guilty, that was that! They had no chance of a fair trial, even if their case went to court.

Q What was the punishment for being drunk?

A Drunkards were made to walk around the town wearing a wooden barrel with holes for their heads and arms. This peculiar costume was called a 'drunkard's cloak'. Its aim was to shame drunks into mending their ways.

A 'cat-o'-nine tails' was a whip made of nine knotted, leather cords which were tied to a short handle.

A special official, called the Witch Finder General, was appointed to hunt witches down. People were terrified of the Witch Finder General.

Q What was a ducking stool?

A A ducking stool was a wooden chair, fixed to the end of a long beam. The victim, usually a woman accused simply of nagging, was held in the chair by a band of iron. Then she was ducked into a pond or river however many times the magistrate stated.

The woman was sometimes wheeled through the streets first, to be jeered at.

Q Who was hung, drawn and quartered?

A Being hung, drawn and quartered was the most horrible form of punishment for traitors. The victim was hanged, then cut down while still alive. He had his insides cut out and his body cut into four!

Q Was witchcraft a crime?

A In the 16th and 17th centuries, people were very superstitious. They were terrified of witches, who were thought to be in league with the devil. Witchcraft was considered one of the most serious of all crimes. Anyone even suspected of being a witch was hunted down, tried and put to death by hanging or burning at the stake. The vast majority of these so-called witches were innocent.

Q How did people know that someone was a witch?

A They didn't because very few people were in fact witches. But they made up ways of identifying witches. Any quite natural marks on an accused woman's body, such as scars, moles or birthmarks were seen as 'witches' marks' and the woman was found guilty.

Tickets were issued inviting people to watch criminals being hanged. In fact, public hangings were very popular spectacles.

When were the gallows used?

In the 18th and 19th centuries, more and more crimes, even quite minor ones, were punished by the death penalty. Other dangers lurked, too. Highwaymen and pirates made travel by land or sea a risky business.

Q Where were people hanged?

A People were hanged on wooden posts, called gallows. In the 18th century, criminals were often gibbeted after being hanged. Their bodies were taken down from the gallows, put in iron cages and hung up in a public place, such as a busy roadside or market place, to frighten other criminals into mending their ways!

Q Who was Dick Turpin?

A Dick Turpin was the most famous of the highwaymen who terrorised the roads in the 18th century. They held up stage-coaches and robbed travellers of their money and jewels. Dick Turpin was finally arrested and hanged.

Q What was a chain gang?

A In the USA, 19th-century prisoners were put to work building roads and railways. They were known as chain gangs because they were chained together by their ankles, to stop them escaping.

Prisoners were set to work 'picking oakum'. This meant picking apart the strands of tarred, twisted ropes. It was very painful on the fingers.

One of the cruellest pirate punishments was to stuff the offender's mouth with oakum, and then set light to it.

Q Why were some criminals sent to other countries, far away?

A Some criminals were sent from Europe to the USA, Australia and South America to serve their sentences. Between 1787 and 1868, some 160,000 convicts sailed from England to Australia. Many died on the eight-month long journey. If they survived and finished their sentences, they stayed and settled in Australia. Many criminals chose to be transported (sent abroad) rather than be hanged.

Q Why were people so afraid of pirates?

A Pirates sailed the seas on the look out for ships to plunder. They thought nothing of killing anyone who stood in their way. But, amongst themselves, they had their own strict code of law and order. If a pirate stole from a fellow-pirate, he was marooned on a desert island.

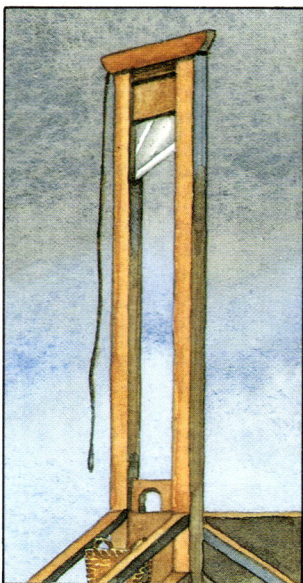

The guillotine was still used in France until 1977.

Q What was a guillotine?

A A guillotine was a machine used for cutting people's heads off. It became very popular in France during the French Revolution in 1789. Many people who opposed the revolution were guillotined, including King Louis XVI and his wife, Marie Antoinette.

Q What was a treadmill?

A A treadmill was a huge wheel with steps on it. You walked from step to step to turn the wheel round. In the 19th century, prisoners had to spend hours at a time on the treadmill. It was exhausting, boring and soul-destroying. The idea was to put prisoners off ever committing a crime again.

A 'king's ransom' means a huge amount of money, enough to secure the release of a person even as important as a king.

How is crime punished today?

Today, criminals are punished in various ways depending on how serious their crimes are. In some countries, the death penalty is still used for the most serious crimes, such as murder. Other types of punishment include prison sentences, fines and community service.

Q Which are the most serious crimes?

A These are murder, burglary, fraud (cheating people out of money), kidnapping and assault. Any crimes which involve violence are treated as very serious.

Q What is a life sentence?

A A life sentence is a very long prison sentence served by the most serious criminals. A criminal may spend the whole of the rest of his or her life in prison.

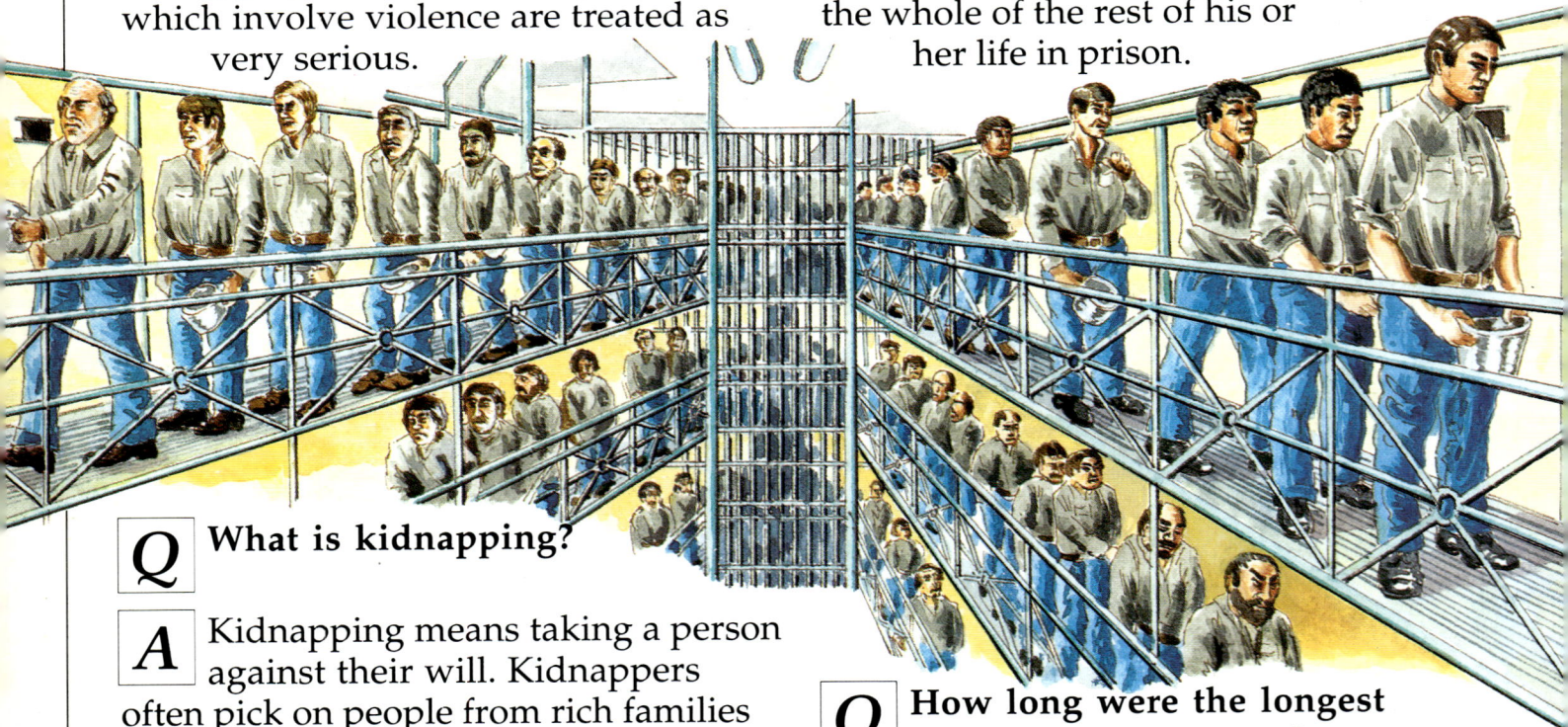

Q What is kidnapping?

A Kidnapping means taking a person against their will. Kidnappers often pick on people from rich families and demand money for their release. This money is called a ransom. Animals are at risk, too. In 1983, the world's top racehorse, Shergar, was kidnapped in Ireland. He was never to be seen again.

Q How long were the longest prison sentences ever?

A In 1989, a woman in Thailand was found guilty of swindling the public out of millions of pounds and sentenced to a total of 141,078 years in prison! In 1972, a sentence of 384,912 years was asked for at the trial of a Spanish postman. He was found guilty of failing to deliver over 40,000 letters.

Community service means working in the community, doing odd jobs and helping children and old people.

Q What is capital punishment?

A Capital punishment means the death penalty given as punishment for the most serious crimes, such as murder. Many countries no longer use capital punishment. Those that do include the USA, China, Iran, Malaysia and South Africa. In Britain, the death penalty was abolished in 1969.

Electric chair

Q What was the heaviest fine ever paid?

A Instead of being sent to prison, some criminals have to pay a fine to the court. Small fines are imposed for minor crimes. But fines for more serious crimes can be very large indeed. In 1988, an American company was found guilty of trading illegally and forced to pay a huge fine of over £300 million.

Q What is a political prisoner?

A In some countries, people can be sent to prison if they disagree with the way the government is running the country. The most famous political prisoner of recent times was Nelson Mandela, who was elected president of South Africa in 1994. He was sentenced to life imprisonment in 1964, and finally released in 1990 after spending 26 years in prison.

The Gunpowder Plot is remembered each year on 5 November, with bonfires and firework displays.

Some criminals have gone down in history for their ruthlessness and cunning, or for their notorious lifestyles. Here you can read about some of the most famous, or infamous, criminals of them all.

Q What was the Gunpowder Plot?

A The Gunpowder Plot was a plot to blow up the Houses of Parliament in London on 5 November 1605. Several barrels of gunpowder were hidden in readiness underneath the Houses of Parliament. The plot was discovered just in time and its ringleaders arrested and executed. The most famous of them was Guy Fawkes.

Q Who was the man in the iron mask?

A The man in the iron mask became famous in a novel by the French writer, Alexandre Dumas. The story was based on a real prisoner, although no one knew his true identity. He was arrested in 1669 and spent 34 years in the Bastille prison, Paris. His face was always hidden by a mask of velvet, not iron. One rumour had it that he was King Louis XIV's twin brother.

Q What is the Mob?

A The Mob is the nickname of the Mafia, the largest criminal organisation in the world. The Mafia began in Sicily, Italy, in the 1800s and soon spread to the USA where it is still in existence. The heads of the various Mafia groups, or 'families', are very powerful indeed.

Wanted posters were put up in an effort to catch the most dangerous criminals. Rewards were offered for their capture.

Q What was the James Gang famous for?

A Frank and Jesse James and their rebel gang were famous for holding up trains. They lived in the USA in the 19th century. No one could catch them, even though huge rewards were offered for their arrest. In 1882, a supposed friend was paid to shoot Jesse. Frank gave himself up but was later freed.

Q Who were Bonnie and Clyde?

A Bonnie and Clyde were two of the most wanted criminals in the USA during the 1930s. They travelled from state to state, stealing money and cars and living in style until the money ran out. Then they stole more. The police finally managed to ambush their car and fired 167 shots into it. This time, even Bonnie and Clyde could not escape.

Bonnie and Clyde

Jesse James

Ned Kelly

Al Capone

Q What were gangsters?

A Gangsters were ruthless criminals who terrorised American cities, such as New York and Chicago, in the 1920s. They made money from gambling, blackmail and selling drugs. One of the most famous gangsters was Al 'Scarface' Capone. His gang was based in Chicago.

Q Where did Ned Kelly live?

A Ned Kelly lived in Australia in the 19th century. He was the last of the 'bushrangers', outlaws who stole from rich settlers in the Australian bush. Ned Kelly became such a hero that no one would turn him in. He was finally caught and hanged in 1880, aged just 25. His last words were 'Such is life'!

One way of identifying a real Leonardo is to look for the artist's fingerprints on the paint. Leonardo often smoothed the paint with his fingers.

A con-artist is someone who tries to trick or deceive other people. This may mean selling fake works of art or producing forged money. It may mean pretending to be someone else. Some of the greatest criminals of all time have been forgers, fakers and imposters.

Keating worked hard to make his fakes look real. He faked mildew stains on very old paintings by wetting the paper and sprinkling coffee granules on it.

Q Who was the greatest forger of art this century?

A The greatest art forger this century was probably a British artist, Tom Keating. For over 25 years, he fooled experts and critics all over the world. He painted 2,500 pictures, all of them fakes, in the style of great artists, such as Renoir, Monet and Van Gogh.

Q What is a forgery?

A A forgery is a fake painting, a banknote or coin, a document such as a passport, or any other object which has been deliberately made to trick people into thinking it is the real thing.

Q How many Mona Lisas are there?

A The Mona Lisa by Leonardo da Vinci is the world's most famous painting. The original hangs in the Louvre Museum in Paris. In 1911, the year the Mona Lisa was stolen, six copies appeared. People paid huge sums of money for them. Today, there are about 60 fakes in existence.

In 1925, a Scotsman, Arthur Ferguson, sold Buckingham Palace, Big Ben and Nelson's Column in London to some American tourists. Not that they were his to sell, of course.

Q How can you spot a forged banknote?

A Some forged banknotes are so good that they are almost impossible to tell from the real thing. To cut down the risk of forgeries, real banknotes have special watermarks and serial numbers which do not appear on fake notes. The actual design of the banknotes also changes from time to time, to make them difficult to copy.

You can see the watermark if you hold a banknote up to the light.

Q Who was Ferdinand Waldo Demara?

A Good question! Ferdinand Waldo Demara spent most of his life pretending to be someone else — a monk, a teacher, a prison officer and even a surgeon. Although he had no medical training at all, he turned out to be a brilliant surgeon. He was only found out because a newspaper reported his success.

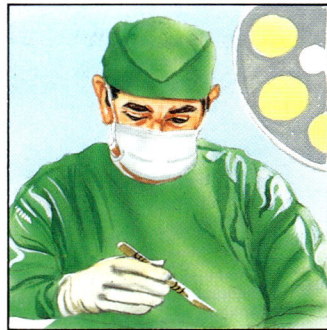

Q How are forgers found out?

A Forgers of paintings and other works of art are often found out because they have used the wrong materials. Any paint, clay or ink must match the type and age of the materials used by the original artist. This sculpture was made in Italy in 1918. The forgers claimed it was made in the 5th century BC. They were only caught out because they used a pigment (colour) not known at that time.

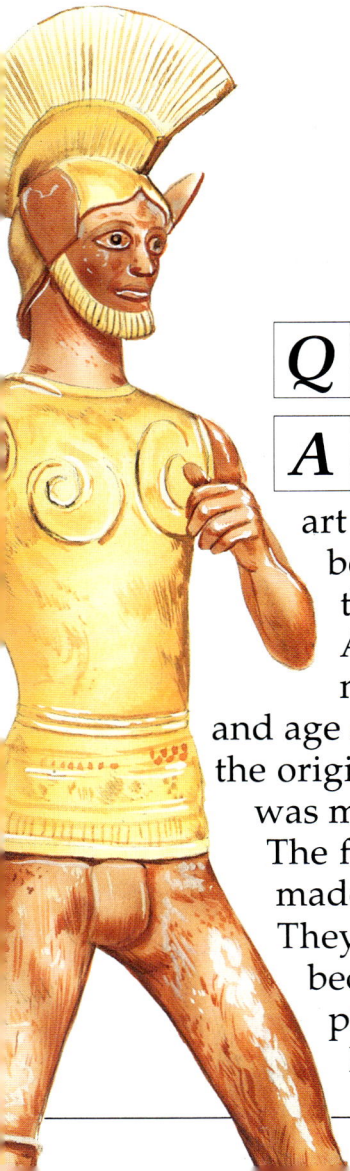

Q Who sold the Eiffel Tower?

A In the 1920s, a con-man, Count Victor Lustig, tried to sell the Eiffel Tower for scrap. The tower is made of thousands of tonnes of valuable steel. By the time he was caught he had sold the tower twice and was trying his luck a third time.

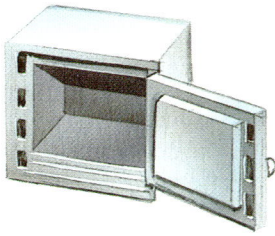

Which are the most famous thefts?

Some criminals specialise in theft or burglary. Some burgle houses or shops. Others work on a much grander scale, stealing priceless jewels and works of art, or robbing banks. If a thief is caught, he or she faces a prison sentence, or at least a heavy fine.

Q What is a cat burglar?

A A cat burglar is a thief who works under cover of night and enters houses by climbing through the windows. He or she moves as quietly and stealthily as a prowling cat.

Q Who tried to steal the Crown Jewels?

A Since the 14th century, the Crown Jewels of England have been kept in the Tower of London. In 1671, Colonel Thomas Blood led a daring attempt to steal them. He and his gang forced their way past the keeper of the jewels, and grabbed the priceless crown, orb and sceptre. They almost got away with it, but were caught when Colonel Blood's horse slipped.

Q Who were the most successful bank robbers?

A In April 1945, thieves stole gold bars worth £3,000 million from the German Reichsbank (national bank). It was the world's largest ever robbery.

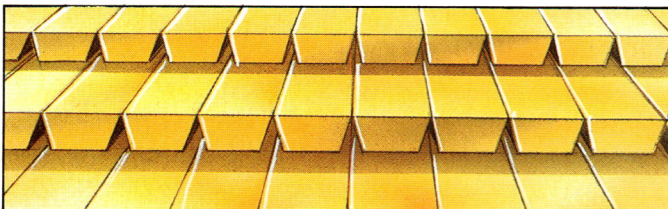

A car thief in Taiwan trained a carrier pigeon to carry ransom money back to him. The pigeon always flew off before the police could catch it.

Q What was one of the easiest thefts?

A In February 1994, thieves stole *The Scream*, a famous painting by Edvard Munch, from the National Gallery in Oslo, Norway. Due to a lapse in security they simply climbed up a ladder, in through a window, and took the painting.

The painting has now been recovered.

Q What is the most valuable thing ever stolen?

A The *Mona Lisa* is a priceless painting. It was stolen from the Louvre in Paris in 1911 by a thief called Vincenzo Perugia. He smuggled the painting out under his clothes and kept it under his bed for the next two years.

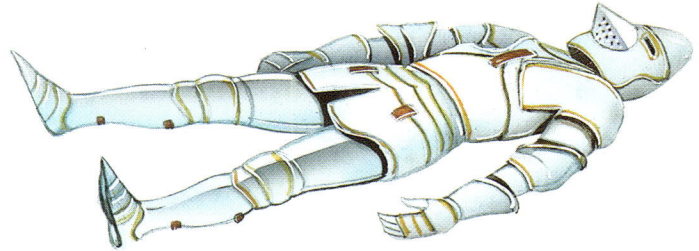

Q Who was the least successful burglar?

A In 1933, a French burglar set off to rob a house, wearing a suit of armour for disguise. It was not a great success. The armour clanked so loudly it woke the house owner up. He pushed the burglar over and called the police. The armour was so heavy that the burglar could not even get to his feet, let alone escape.

Q What was the Great Train Robbery?

A The Great Train Robbery happened at about 3 am on 8 August 1963. Robbers held up a mail train, travelling from Glasgow to London, and got away with £2.5 million pounds in used banknotes (worth about £25 million in today's money). Very little of the loot was ever recovered. Most of the robbers were eventually caught.

How are criminals caught?

Before America had a proper police force, sheriffs and marshalls kept law and order. They wore badges like the one on the left.

Some criminals confess to their crimes or are caught red-handed at the scene of the crime. Many, however, have to be tracked down by the police. This can involve months of detective work, looking for clues and interviewing suspects and witnesses before someone is charged with the crime and the case can go to court.

Q Where was the first police force?

A One of the first police forces was formed in Ancient Rome by Emperor Augustus in AD 6. It was known as the *Cohortes Vigilum*. It also acted as the fire brigade.

Cohortes Vigilum

Today's policemen and women may be uniformed or wear plain clothes to avoid being recognised.

Q Why did people raise a hue and cry?

A Hue and cry was a way of catching criminals in the Middle Ages. The people of the district in which a crime was committed were punished for it, unless they raised the hue and cry. This meant chasing after criminals and catching them within 40 days.

Q When was the first modern police force formed?

A The first modern police force was set up in 1749 in London. The constables were known as the Bow Street Runners because their headquarters were in Bow Street. The runners were extremely successful, helping to rid the streets of London of robbers and highwaymen. They wore ordinary clothes and carried handcuffs, pistols and wooden batons.

Q What is Interpol?

A Interpol stands for the International Criminal Police Organisation. It was founded in 1923 to help police from different countries deal with international criminals. In its headquarters in Paris, Interpol has an international register of criminals and huge fingerprint file. More than 120 countries now belong to Interpol.

Handcuffs are sometimes used to stop suspected criminals escaping.

Q What job did a thief-taker do?

A In the 18th century, the government offered large rewards of money to people who helped them catch criminals. Some people, known as thief-takers, made a living from catching criminals. The thief-takers were often criminals themselves who turned in their friends for money. For their troubles, they got £40 per criminal and the criminal's horse or weapons.

Q What is the scene of the crime?

A The scene of the crime is the place where a crime has been committed. It could be a house, a road, a bank or shop, a field, anywhere in fact. The first part of a police investigation is to search the scene of the crime thoroughly for clues. They may be helped by sniffer dogs.

Q What are clues?

A Clues are anything which help the police track down criminals and solve crimes. Clues include anything from fingerprints, hair and scraps of clothing, to eyewitness reports and anybody acting in a suspicious or unusual manner.

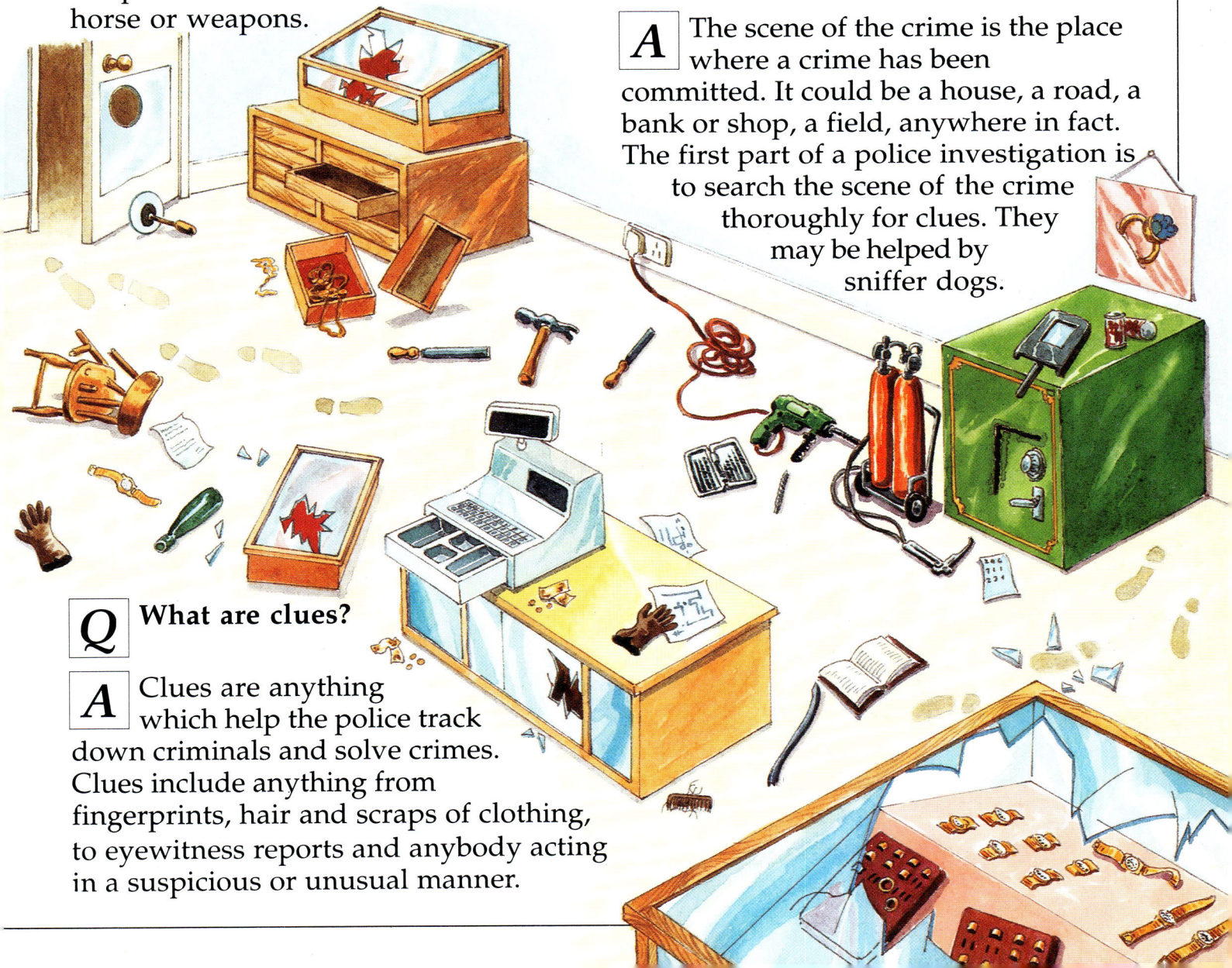

In 1942, a murder case in America was solved by a parrot. The police heard it squawking the name of the murderer.

How are crimes solved?

Once the police have enough clues and have collected enough evidence, they may be able to arrest someone on suspicion of having committed a crime. They must interview suspects before they charge them with the crime or let them go free again.

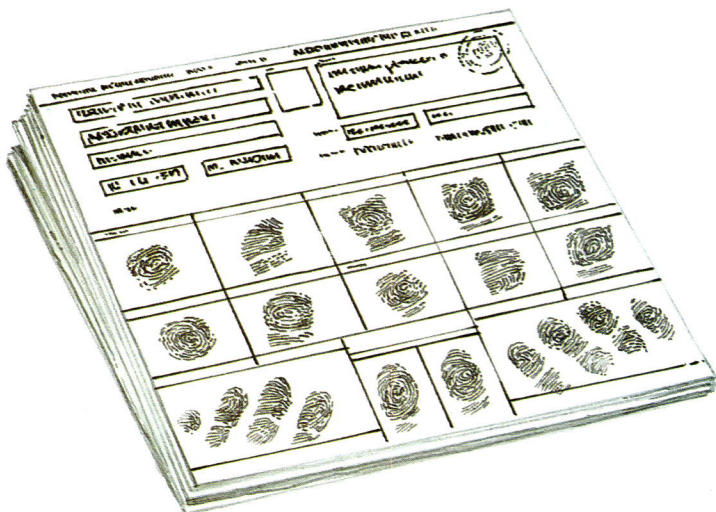

Q Why are suspects questioned?

A A suspect is questioned by the police so they can try to confirm their suspicions about his or her guilt. Some suspects confess to a crime. Others are cleared of any charges and released. If a suspect is charged with a crime, a written account of any interviews is used in court as evidence.

Q Who takes part in an identification parade?

A An identification parade is made up of the suspect and a group of people who look like the suspect. The victim, or witness of a crime, has to see if they can pick out their suspect from the group. There are strict guidelines to prevent cases of mistaken identity.

Q How are fingerprints used to identify criminals?

A The patterns of lines and whirls on your fingertips are called your fingerprints. No two people have exactly the same fingerprints which makes them vital clues. The police keep a register of the prints of known or suspected criminals. If they can match the fingerprints at the scene of a crime with any of those on the register, they can identify the criminal.

Q What is an alibi?

A The word 'alibi' means elsewhere in Latin. It is used to mean that a suspect was somewhere else at the time a crime was committed and so could not be linked to it. The police check all alibis to see if they are true or false.

Footprints are used as clues in places such as Africa where people go barefoot. Everyone has a different pattern of ridges on the soles of the feet.

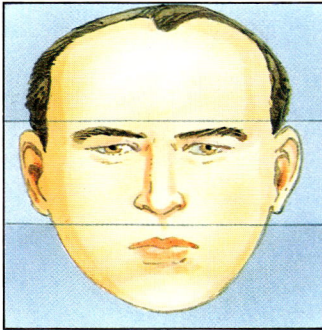

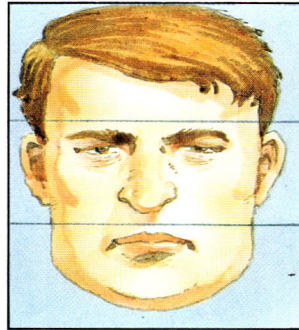

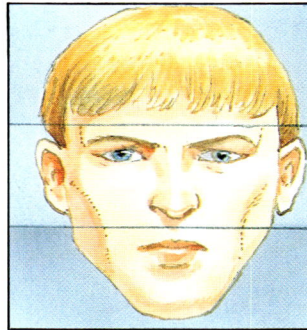

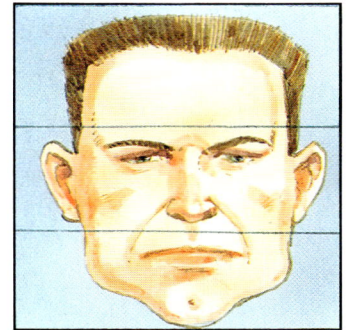

Q What is photofit?

A Photofit is a system which helps victims, or witnesses, identify criminals. They have to pick out photos of features, such as eyes, hair, nose, ears and so on, and build them up into a face. The police also use computer images to build pictures of criminals.

Q How does a lie detector work?

A A lie detector is a machine which records a person's heart rate, breathing rate and blood pressure while he or she is being questioned. These rates usually increase if the person is lying. But they can also rise even if a person is completely innocent, because the situation is so stressful.

Q What does a forensic scientist do?

A A forensic scientist uses scientific techniques and tests to help the police solve crimes. He or she examines clues such as hair, bloodstains and fibres from clothes, identifies bodies, studies bullets and bullet wounds, and also analyses poisons and drugs. Forensic science is a mixture of many different sciences — biology, chemistry, physics and medicine.

How do courts work?

In the past, if they were sentencing someone to death, judges wore square black caps on top of their wigs.

If a suspect is charged with a serious crime, his or her case is then heard in court. This is where the person's guilt or innocence is decided and where the judge decides on the length and style of punishment that the criminal should receive. There are different courts for different crimes.

Q Who would you find in a courtroom?

A Present in the courtroom for a serious crime would be the judge, jury, the accused, barristers acting for and against the accused, witnesses for and against the accused, court officials and members of the general public.

Q What does a jury do?

A The jury, made up of 12 ordinary men and women, listens to all the evidence put before them and then must decide if the accused is guilty or innocent of the crime. The jury's decision is called a verdict.

Q What does the judge do?

A The judge keeps order in the court and passes sentence if the jury finds the accused person guilty. The judge can give the jury information about difficult points of law but has to leave the jury to make its own decision, based on the evidence it has heard.

Witnesses are called to give evidence. They have to swear to tell the truth.

The judge

The jury

The accused

The scales of justice are a symbol of the courts and the legal system.

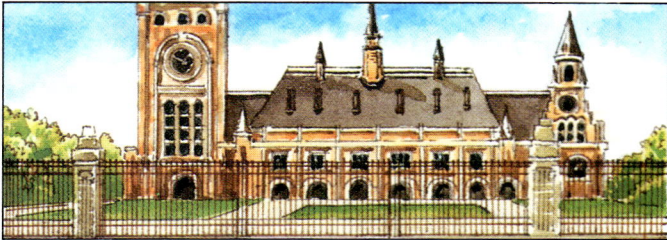

Q Where is the World Court?

A The World Court is another name for the International Court of Justice. It sits in the Hague, Holland. The court has 15 judges, from 15 different countries, elected by the UN (United Nations). It deals with disputes between various countries and with matters of international law.

Q What happens during a cross-examination?

A During a cross-examination, a witness is questioned by the barrister acting for the other side. The barrister tries to get the witness to give evidence which would help his or her particular side of the argument.

Two barristers present the case for and against the accused

Q How were juries picked in Ancient Greek times?

A In Ancient Greece, people simply went to court and volunteered for jury service. If there were too many volunteers, a machine called a *kleroteria* was used to pick the 200 jurors needed.

The colour of the ball next to a volunteer's name decided whether he would be picked for jury duty that day.

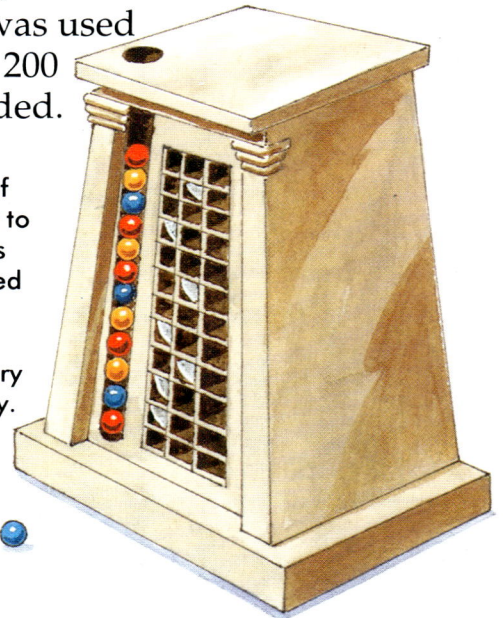

Q Why do judges wear wigs?

A Judges first wore wigs at the end of the 17th century when wigs were a part of everyday dress. Later, they kept the wigs as part of their uniform. They probably felt they helped make them look important.

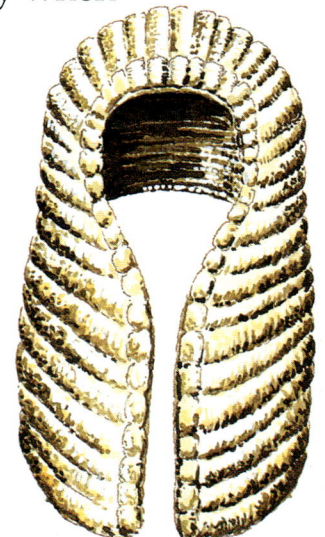

Judges' wigs used to be made of human hair. Today they are made of horse hair or of artificial fibres.

How long are trials?

A trial is the name given to events inside the courtroom, that is, the hearing of the evidence, the jury's verdict and the passing of any sentence. Some trials are quite short and straightforward. Others are longer and more complicated.

Q Which were the longest and shortest trials?

A One of the longest murder trials ever ran for 136 days, from November 1976 to June 1977. The jury in the Old Bailey, London, listened to 3.5 million words of evidence before finding the accused guilty. In contrast, one of the shortest murder trials on record lasted for just 30 seconds.

Q What were men of straw?

A In the Middle Ages, men of straw could be hired to give false evidence at a trial. They got their name from their official badge — a piece of straw sticking out of their shoes.

Q Who was tried at the Nuremberg War Trials?

A The Nuremberg War Trials were held in Germany, in 1945–1946. The accused were all leaders of the German Nazis who had just been defeated in World War II. They were found guilty of various war crimes, including the killing of millions of Jews.

Q Why were the Salem witch trials so unfair?

A In 1692, in Salem, USA, 22 women were found guilty of being witches and hanged. None of them had done anything wrong and all the evidence against them was completely made up. They were innocent victims of a terrible witch-hunt which was sweeping the country at the time.

In Roman trials, the accused person sometimes wore a ragged, dirty toga to make the jury feel sorry for him.

Q Were animals ever put on trial?

A Yes, they were. In the Middle Ages, animals could be tried for all sorts of crimes, from witchcraft to murder. Pigs were often flogged for breaking the law! But snails, worms caterpillars and even flies could be put on trial, too.

Q Could animals ever hope to be let off?

A In 1521, in France, a lawyer managed to get the case against his clients, a group of rats, dropped. The rats were accused of eating the local barley crop. They were let off because the lawyer claimed that they had not been summoned to court properly, and could not attend anyway because the presence of the courtroom cat put their lives in grave danger.

Q Why did a trial have a curse put on it?

A In 1949, a witchdoctor was put on trial in Zimbabwe and sentenced to two years' imprisonment for illegally carrying on his craft. He was so upset he put a curse on the court, saying that the city would soon be overrun with lions. And so it was! For a week or so, a pride of lions terrorised the streets, attacking people and animals.

Prisoners in the Middle Ages had to provide their own food, drink, bedding and candles.

Are all prisons the same?

There are many different types of prison. Criminals guilty of violent or other serious crimes are sent to high-security prisons. Minor criminals may be sent to 'open', or less strict, prisons.

Q How have prisons changed?

A In the Middle Ages, prisoners were often flung into castle dungeons and left to rot! Later, purpose-built prisons were constructed. Prisoners were very badly treated. Many died of disease and overwork. Gradually, prison conditions improved. Criminals are now allowed to study and train for jobs, while being punished.

The Bastille was totally destroyed after the attack.

Q Who was imprisoned in the Tower of London?

A The Tower of London was built as a royal palace. Later, it was used as prison for royal traitors while they waited to be executed on nearby Tower Hill. They arrived at the Tower by boat, entering through 'Traitors' Gate', on the River Thames.

Q Which prison started a revolution?

A On 14 July, 1789, an angry mob stormed the Bastille, a prison in Paris. This was the start of the French Revolution. People saw the prison as a symbol of the king's privilege and power which they wanted to end. There were just seven prisoners inside, not the hundreds the mob had expected.

The Tower of London was built in the 11th century by William the Conqueror.

Prison ships went out of use in the 1850s.

In the 19th century, debtors were sent to prison until their debts were paid. Many spent their whole lives in prison.

Q What were hulks?

A Hulks were old, rotting warships, moored along the coast and used as prisons in the 18th and 19th centuries. Conditions for prisoners on board were terrible. The ships were infested with rats and the food was very poor. Thousands of prisoners were crammed together in a small space.

Q What was the 'Great Escape'?

A The Great Escape is the name given to the daring escape of 76 prisoners during World War II. They secretly tunnelled their way out of a German prisoner-of-war camp. The tunnel took over a year to dig, at a rate of about 12 metres a month.

Q Which was the unluckiest escape?

A In April 1976, 75 prisoners escaped from Saltillo prison in Mexico along a tunnel which had taken them six months to dig. Unfortunately for them, the tunnel came up right inside a nearby courtroom. All 75 men were recaptured and sent straight back to prison!

Q Which was the most secure prison?

A From 1933–1963, Alcatraz, an island in San Francisco Bay, USA, was the site of a maximun security prison, called 'the Rock'. During that time, not a single prisoner escaped. Of the 23 men that tried, six drowned, five were shot dead and 12 were recaptured.

'The Rock' on Alcatraz

Index

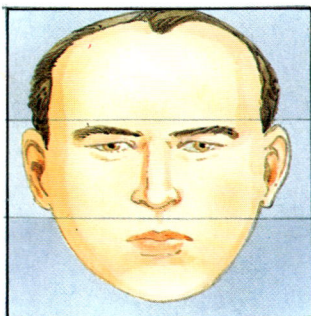

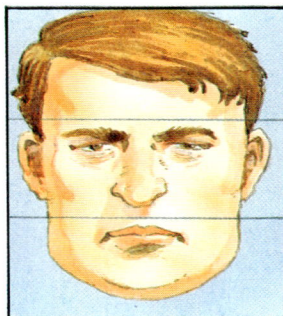

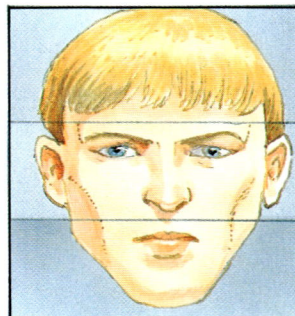

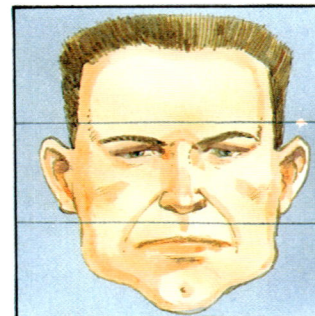